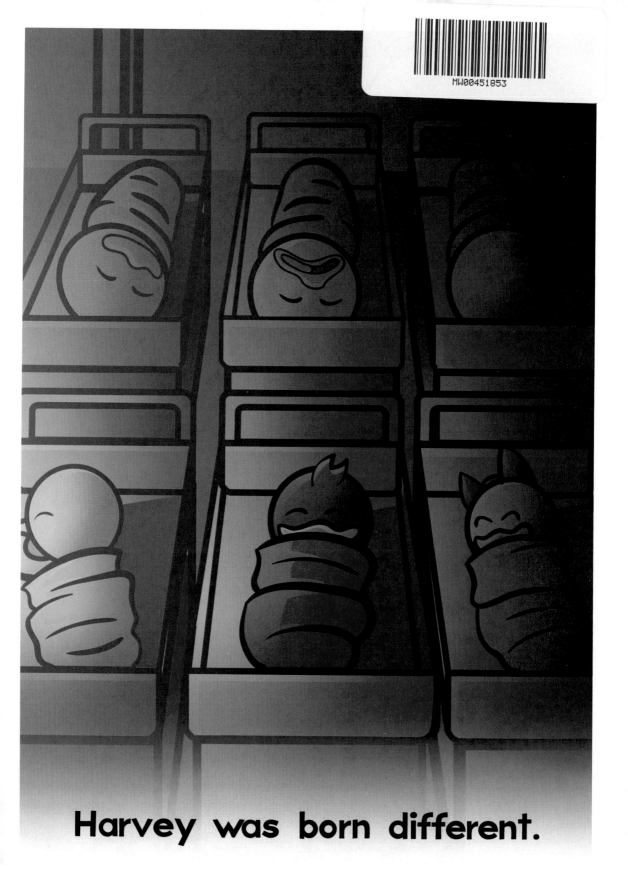

Harvey was born different.

All the other ducks were yellow, but Harvey was born brown!

HARVEY
The Little Brown Duck

Dedicated to London & Maddox "You Can Do It"

Written by JV Harvey
Illustrated by E.Campbell
Edited by Nicole Nicholson

GO HARVEY! GO!!

JVHarvey.com

E.CampbellWORX
about.me/e.campbellworx

And for bookings email...
kreativeinfluence@yahoo.com

HARVEY
The Little Brown Duck

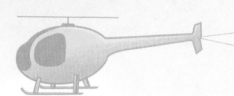

GO HARVEY! GO!!

Coloring Book Section

He always seemed to be
the slowest.

And compared to the other ducks, he was the shortest.

But no matter what, he always had a smile on his face.

When the other ducks
went ice skating, so did
Harvey. He wasn't the
best at it, but he tried.

When the other ducks played basketball, so did Harvey. He missed every shot but still he tried.

But none of the yellow
ducks could dance as well
as Harvey. He danced to
his own beat.

One day, a duck named
Stan got stuck in a log.

None of the other ducks could fit into the log. Who can rescue Stan?

"Hurry up and go get Harvey. He will be the perfect size."

Harvey knew just what to do. Wasting no time he found a rope, pushed it into the log, and made sure Stan was holding on.

All the ducks helped pull
Stan out to safety.

Suddenly the little brown duck, who was so different from all the other ducks became an instant star.

Teaching everyone it's OK
to be different just never
give up!

Harvey The Little Brown Duck!